Autistic, Middle-Aged, and Asian

A How-To Guide for Women Kinda, But Not Really, Exactly Like Me

Dr. Sefi Corner, A Professional Mask

Calm Corner Publishing

ISBN: 9798847740913
Imprint: Independently published
Cover design by: S. Corner
Published in the United States of America

THIS IS AN E-BOOK IN PAPERBACK FORM

Please note that this book was written as a short e-book and allowed to be printed in paperback form to make the e-book accessible to everyone.

CONTENTS

1 INTRODUCTION

Autism is only beginning to be understood, autism in women is even less understood. Autism in women who are middle-aged has even less information.

This e-book is written by a middle-aged woman on the autistic spectrum for other people who identify with being a middle-aged woman on the autistic spectrum. As a middle-aged woman, I found that there's a severe lack of information about people like me and that makes me feel like there aren't many people out there like me. Except that can't be true just based on the sheer number of people there are on this planet! I'm pretty sure there are lots of middle-aged women with autism out there in the world and I wrote this book so that I can find them. You. So that I can find you. So that I can learn more about you, and maybe I can learn more about myself.

I hope you find this e-book useful as well as funny because I'm a funny person and I find the life I'm in rather funny. Granted, you are reading a book written by an actual autistic person and what I find funny might not be funny to you.

This short e-book is nonfiction and based on how my brain works. If I ever write a full book, I will be sure to insert all the research I've done that has gone into writing this e-book. I am indeed one of those autistic people who turned a special interest into a career. In my case, I turned a lifetime interest in teaching into a career as an educator, learner, and researcher in education. That said, I am not a neuroscientist. I am a professional educator with a focus on how children learn. But, along the way, I have learned a lot about my brain as well as other autistic brains. This e-book is based on the experience of one person on the autism spectrum.

Who is this person? I am a 44-year-old woman with autism. I am also an Asian woman. I live in the suburbs of the United States. Right now, I am very much upper middle class, though I was raised lower class, which is to say, I was so poor, I had holes in my shoes for most of my childhood. In third grade, I was identified as gifted. I was told that I scored near genius-level. I wondered which questions made me miss the genius mark. In middle school, I was identified as having special needs, though not specifically on the autism spectrum. My teachers called me the absentminded professor.

Colloquially, that means I am considered "twice exceptional" as well as "high functioning". I do not like either term because, depending on the situation, I can be exceptionally "low functioning".

Our Brains as Constellations

As you read this e-book, keep in mind this one phrase that I've come across. If you've met one person with autism, you have met… one person with autism.

I like to imagine the human brain as a sky full of stars. When we look out at the night sky, we see patterns emerge and call them constellations. The well-known constellations are what I identify as neurotypical. Those are typical patterns of behaviors, characteristics, preferences, and norms. The well-known constellations are made up of different stars and galaxies, and there are many constellations. That's what most people are: a well-known constellation of typical patterns of behaviors, characteristics, preferences, and norms. In this e-book, I will follow the current convention of calling them neurotypical.

People with autism have different, perhaps lesser known, constellations made up of the same universe of stars and galaxies. Different patterns emerge from our characteristics.

My constellation might not be the same as yours. But we are all made up of beautiful stars.

2 HOW TO KNOW IF YOU HAVE AUTISM

If you are a woman and especially if you are a middle-aged woman, chances are you are not professionally identified as having autism. Research into autism has historically been done with White, male children. Male children are more likely to be identified than female children. Adults are even less likely to be identified. So, how do you know if you have autism if you are a woman and especially if you are older?

Right now, in the United States, it is expensive, laborious, and time-consuming to seek an autistic diagnosis as an adult. The decision to seek an official diagnosis is up to you. Some people seek the diagnosis as it can give them access to supports and services that would otherwise be out of reach. Others seek a diagnosis so that it can give them peace of mind and a sense of relief to have answers to many of their life's burning questions.

Am I Faking It?

One sad, but common, reason why adults seek an official diagnosis is because some people believe that unless you are identified as having autism, then you are faking it. These doubters may be strangers, co-workers, bosses, family members, and friends. But these doubters might also be the individuals who suspect that they have autism. You. You may be wondering if you're faking it, while a sense of uncertainty and disquiet grows within you every day.

So, let's get into it. If you suspect you have autism or that you are on the autism spectrum, you can indeed seek professional identification. Some people have found that being professionally identified has reassured them and makes them feel better and safer. If you have that option, then I encourage you to seek professional identification.

Not everyone has that option. There are other ways of checking to see if you are on the autism spectrum if you suspect that you are.

Growing up in an Asian family, my parents and

other relatives called me crazy and strange. That was my first clue. Those were literally their words, "crazy" and "strange", except in Vietnamese and not in English. A Southeast Asian family with little formal education does not have words to describe people with autism. This was also back in the early 80s. This was when autism was gaining awareness in the American media.

In third grade, I was identified as being gifted and highly intelligent! That helped my family explain some of my characteristics, behaviors, and outbursts. From then on, they believed that I was a crazy genius. Those were also literally their words, "crazy genius".

In middle-school, my English teacher decided that an eighth grader who never talked in class was a sign that there was something else going on. She made it her business to get me the support I needed.

Of course, this had happened before. In second grade, I was not verbal at all. My teacher attributed that to me being a shy Asian girl. She didn't wonder why I wasn't shy in first grade or in third grade. She was also the one who yelled at me "YOU TALK TOO MUCH! BE QUIET!" at the beginning of second grade and didn't notice that I stopped talking the rest of the year.

In eighth grade, my English teacher referred me to special education and the school team determined and identified that I did indeed need special education support. I don't remember what my specific diagnosis was. I highly doubt it was autism. My grandmother, who was my caretaker at the time, wasn't literate in English, and I wasn't very proficient in Vietnamese. She had difficulty explaining to me what was going on. By the end of eighth grade, I knew that I was gifted and special.

That helped me deal with some of my feelings of being an alien on the wrong planet. And if you have autism, chances are, you know exactly what I mean when I say, "being an alien on the wrong planet".

In 1996, I entered college and got access to this thing called the Internet. A family member, my cousin Belle, told me that there was a very good chance I had Asperger's and sent me an online quiz just to see where I was in that inventory. I was shocked. I was enthralled. I was intrigued. I took the inventory and it placed me firmly in the territory of having Asperger's.

Here's a side note if you haven't heard of Asperger's before. It used to be that Asperger's

Syndrome was diagnosed separately from autism spectrum disorder (ASD). It was thought that people with Asperger's were different and higher functioning. Nowadays, the term Asperger's is still commonly used, but clinically everyone is placed on the autism spectrum.

I felt shook up after taking that inventory. I now have a term for what I may be, but I didn't quite believe it. I kept hoping it was a joke that I may have Asperger's. I hoped that I was just a strange person. Five years later, I took a different inventory online, and it once again indicated that I was likely on the autism spectrum. And then a few years after that, I took another inventory, and guess what? It indicated that I was on the autism spectrum. Every few years after that, I took an entirely different assessment online, and guess what? They always indicated that I was on the autism spectrum. Recently, I took yet another online self-assessment, and it again indicated that I was very likely on the autism spectrum. I think by now, I've done enough, and I quite believe that I am indeed on the autism spectrum. Will I take yet another self-assessment online in a few years? Yes, yes indeed, I will.

Every time I take one of these assessments, a part of me hopes that it will say something different. I believe that's because I haven't yet fully accepted.

Somewhere deep in my head I believe that I am faking it. That is something I am still working on within myself.

If you suspect that you are on the autism spectrum, do what you need to do for you to feel comfortable and confident about yourself. If you think that you need a professional diagnosis, go seek it out. If you think that a self-assessment is sufficient, then it absolutely is. If you suspect that you are, and you are crying as you read this, then you are, and that is OK too. I'm glad to have found you.

3 MASKING: HOW TO MIMIC LIKE A PRO

In college, I had an interesting conversation with my best friend, Renata. Not surprisingly, I had a lot of social difficulties. People did not behave in a way that made sense to me. People behaved in a way that frustrated me. People did not react to me in a way that I thought was appropriate or logical. To put it another way, I did not like people, and I don't think they liked me either.

I remember Renata had some friends hanging out in our dorm room one evening. They were mutual acquaintances. We had a good time chatting and joking around. I was laughing. They were laughing. I had a fantastic time! At 9pm, I opened the door and said, "Good night! Thank you for coming!"

Renata was so mad at me. She said I kicked them

out! That I was being rude!

Excuse me, I was not being rude. They were being rude for not leaving before 9pm on a school night! What were they thinking?!

Dating was the worst. I was not interested in dating during high school. I wasn't really interested in college either. My friends, the few of them that I did have, thought I was being silly, or rather, that I was being judgmental and prudish. Honestly, I just was not interested.

Dating was the worst of the worst. I watched my friends flirt and go on dates, quite successfully. While I was not interested, I thought I should at least participate and pretend to be like them. I tried flirting on my own at first, to some spectacularly awkward results.

I remember this cute boy in my computer science class. I thought I would give flirting a try with him. I started by staring at him intensely when we had a study session. For hours. Or at least what felt like hours. He did not seem to appreciate that.

When I told my friends, they laughed and said that is not how girls flirt. We were very sexist back then. So I asked, "Well, how do you flirt then?"

They each launched into the different ways that they flirted, and some commonalities came out. I pointed out that they seem to be following the same script. They exclaimed, "That's it! You just follow these rules, and you're flirting. The boys fall for it every time!"

One of the girls later came out as lesbian, which was extremely brave for an Asian girl at the time, and I quite admired her for it. I also admired the fact that she was equally successful dating women. I could only assume that the girls fell for the same script too? Or maybe she changed scripts.

I gave myself a new homework assignment: study flirting, study people who flirt, and write a script for myself. I spent one semester at college doing just that.

Then, I executed my new script on the same cute boy from computer science. The next time he knocked on my door for a study session, I opened my door, tilted my head, smiled at him shyly, and looked at him through my lashes and bangs. About a week later, he invited me to go to a club together.

Here, I want to point out that I did not realize that he was asking me out on a date. I only figured out it was a date afterward when I was getting dressed and Renata brought a pack of girls to fuss over me. They even tweezed my eyebrows. That was a big clue.

The cute boy and I went to the club and danced together all night, at which he sweated all over me. Gross. I avoided him after that, poor kid. No more study sessions with him. Taking me to a club was a bad choice on his part, anyway, seeing as how it was sensory hell for me. Sweating on me did not help matters.

Women with autism present differently from men with autism, that is to say, they exhibit patterns of behaviors differently from men with autism. Research is not clear on whether it's because there are actual differences or because, in Western culture, women have been taught to behave differently. While many people with autism mask, women have a tendency to mimic behaviors and expectations around them more than men. Let me repeat that, women with autism have a stronger tendency to mimic and mask natural behaviors and tendencies based on other people's behaviors and expectations.

I learned in college that to be successful in this alien world in which people don't leave your room before 9pm on a weeknight as they should, I had to observe the aliens around me and copy their behavior. I do it so well and successfully that I now present as a somewhat awkward and intense, but highly intelligent, professional woman. My work persona is what I call a "professional mask". She is a character I play just as much as this new character I've invented, the autistic author Dr. Sefi Corner.

The ability to purposefully mask our natural behaviors and tendencies can be a power and a problem. One problem with masking is that it drains a person's mental and emotional energy. Simply trying to navigate a neurotypical world is exhausting, leaving little energy to do anything else.

At the simplest level, I have to refrain myself from kicking visitors out of the house at 9pm and continue socializing with them even after I have gone past my comfort level. Just so I'm not considered rude.

I have to refrain from rocking back and forth when I'm sitting in a chair in a room with other people, even though rocking back and forth feels good and sitting still feels like there's a rod shoved up my back.

I have to say, "Hello! How are you?" to people I

meet even though I honestly can't care less about how they're doing, and when asked how I'm doing, I'm supposed to say "Great! How are you?" instead of the truth which might be "Terrible! I didn't sleep last because the room was 2 degrees too warm!"

Another problem with masking is that you are not sure who you are, who your authentic self is, and you end up with self-esteem issues stemming from insecurities, uncertainties about who you are, and what you actually want out of life. This can lead to many mental health issues, including depression and anxiety.

What does this mean to a middle-aged woman with autism? It means that there's a good chance you are already masking. It means that very likely you have been watching the people around you all of your life and you have been pretending and copying behaviors that you see around you in order to fit in or to ease your way in the neurotypical social world. It also means that you might not be aware that you are doing this, nor aware that it is a fairly common behavior in women with autism. It might also mean you have self-esteem issues and questions about who you are.

Now, knowing that women with autism have strong tendencies to be mask, think about how you can use it as a tool. A tool is something that you can use when you want to, pick it up when you need it, and put it down when you don't. Consider ways that you can use masking, or mimicry, in your life intentionally, make decisions about when you want to mimic a specific behavior when you need to for a specific reason, and decide when you know longer need to. Using masking as a tool intentionally will help you get a better sense of who you are. It also means you know who you are when you behave a certain way and when you don't. Being able to stop masking when you need to will help you take care of your mental and emotional self, preserving your energy for when you need to expend it under difficult situations.

In which situations have I been successful using masking? Dating for one. I am outrageously good at dating and flirting. Professionally, I am also an outrageously effective presenter. I have presented to crowds of hundreds of people and have them eating out of my hands. I mask with my in-laws. My in-laws know a version of me that is a delightful individual, funny, gentle, calm, and patient. They don't know any other version of me other than the one I choose to show them. I have many versions.

How do I do this? I study the people around me, in traditional media and in social media, at work, at the grocery store, at the doctor's office. Everywhere. I find common behaviors and expectations. When I was younger, I would write down little behavior scripts on my computer. I would write down scenarios of what would happen, both the dialogues and physical movements that I would need under different circumstances. I would mentally rehearse the scripts over and over again until I internalized them. For presentations, I would literally rehearse in front of a mirror. Decades later, I have a large collection of mental scripts I have developed over the years. I don't need to write them down anymore.

4 HOW TO SPIN YOUR SPECIAL INTERESTS AND HOW MANY CAN YOU HAVE AT ONE TIME

I can talk all day about three topics: my husband, my dogs, my brain, and education, especially social justice in education. Try to have a conversation with me about anything else. It used to be that I would turn my back and walk away. I was just not interested. It took Renata a lot of work to convince me to stand there and just listen to people, and eventually I learned how to pretend as if I was interested in what they were talking about. But honestly, I'm usually not interested.

Everyone has special interests, whether they are neurotypical or autistic. A typical person may have a hobby, a collection, a life-long pursuit, a beloved sport, and so forth. Their interests may change with time or may ebb and flow. People with autism have special interests, otherwise known as SPINs within the autistic community. The SPINS may also change with time or ebb and flow. However, SPINs are qualitatively different from a typical person's interest. The level of focus is different. The intensity is different.

When I have a special interest, I completely absorb myself in it. I read all about it, watch all the YouTubes, collect all the magazines, and download all the podcasts. I want to think about my SPIN, talk about my SPIN, and write about my SPIN. This is why this e-book exists. My gifted, autistic brain is a special interest of mine.

When I was younger, I would get mad if someone interrupts me when I'm deeply involved in my SPIN, which is all the time. I would get irritated if someone tried to distract me or talk to me about nonessential matters, which is everything that's not one of my SPINs. SPINs are different from a typical person's hobby.

A person with autism would find a special special joy in their special interest. There is just no rush like being able to indulge in and share your special interest with someone else. People outside of the autistic community may consider it an obsession. Certainly, many people I've talked to consider it annoying that I might dump information on them.

My son would make sure I'm not around before talking to his dad, "Is mom around? I want to talk about my social studies class but I don't want to get her mad." I'm not mad! It's not my fault that the teacher's wrong and I can list in detail the twenty reasons why they're wrong!

For a person with autism and a SPIN, there's nothing better in life than to talk about their special interest to someone who would listen for hours at a time. That's why I make sure to go to education conferences. It's my chance to indulge in my special interest for an entire week with people who want to raptly listen to me.

As with every research area on autism, there's not a lot of research about special interests among adult women. We do have research that focuses on children's special interests. A lot of the special interests involve colors, textures, puzzles, cars, and things like that. That list tells me that the research included children with autism who identify as boys in a Western culture. These special interests are also easily observable by the adults around them.

Can special interests be of topics that are far less observable? I believe the answer is absolutely yes. I believe that people with autism who identify as women have a stronger tendency to have special interests that are more abstract and unobservable but no less involving or worthy of hours-long conversations.

All my life, I have been interested in education. By the age of seven I knew I was going to be a teacher. Starting in sixth grade, I started tutoring other children. In ninth grade, I took an afterschool job at a Catholic school as a tutor. For college, I chose my college based on whether it had a good teachers' college as part of their graduate department. By the age of 21, I was already a credentialed teacher. By the age of 43, I have a doctorate degree in education. And right at this moment, I am writing this book because I want to teach more and share more about autism, and this comes from my interest in all things education.

Over the years, I collected two more special interests. My husband and my two dogs. I like to think of it as three concentric rings of interest. The inner ring consists of my husband, my two dogs, and education. The inner ring does not change much throughout my life. In fact, as you can guess by now, I used to have only one interest in my inner ring, education. I added two more interests later in life. I'm growing as a person, can you tell?

My middle ring consists of interests that come and go throughout my life. For example, currently I am obsessed with the marathon. I spent the last year training and ran my first 26.2 mile race. I've signed up for two more, and I'm excited to start my training in a few weeks. As soon as I got interested in running a marathon, I bought all the magazines, all the shoes, all the shorts, all the tech T-shirts, all the gears you can think of. I watched all the YouTube videos and downloaded and listened to all the podcasts on my run. I immersed myself in running. It's a SPIN that's only one year old. I'm not sure if it's an inner ring special interest yet. I might lose interest. We shall see.

A couple of years ago, I immersed my life in gardening. I bought all the books about gardening, I bought all the seeds, all the soil, all the garden pots, and even worms to enrich the soil. I listened to all the podcasts, I watched all the YouTube videos, and I planted as much as I possibly could. Within three months they all started dying because I did not water them. This is a middle ring level special interest. I know it is a middle ring level special interest because it has gone in and out of my life repeatedly over the years many times. This was not the first time I killed off an entire garden because I lost interest a few months after planting them. I'm pretty sure that in a few years I will be interested in gardening again.

The outer ring of my special interests consists of… Nothing. Absolutely nothing. I don't have any other interests. This is one of the reasons why I know for certain that I am on the autistic spectrum. It is incredibly difficult to get me interested in anything that's not within my two inner rings. It isn't that I get bored. I was never interested in the first place. I just cannot find it within myself. And now I'm OK with that. It's just who I am

I've heard from other people with autism that they have many interests and while others don't have any. Some people have many special interests. Some people have very few interests. Some people, like me, definitely lack interest in anything that's not a special interest. And all of that is OK.

I love sharing my interests with other people. More recently, what I've learned to love is to enjoy other people's interests. I love to hear other people share their special interests with me. It makes me happy to share in their joy, even if I never share in their interests. Whether or not you have a special interest, I hope you are able to make space in your life to listen with rapt attention to someone else share joy in their special interest with you.

5 HOW TO SURVIVE STARBUCKS, THE MALL, AND OTHER SENSORY HELLSPOTS

The first time I went into a Starbucks coffee shop was about 10 years ago with a friend. I hated it!!!!

I walked into a small, crowded, dark, stinky, loud room with terrible acoustics that made no sense whatsoever. I "stood in line", and by that, I mean vaguely standing around a crowd of people for what felt like an eternity to get up to the cashier to order my coffee. There was no obvious place to start getting into line. There's no obvious place to go pick up your coffee, at least not that I could figure out. It was a group of people standing in small little crowds in front of a counter space.

Everyone acted like they knew exactly what to do, and I had no idea what to do, because all the rules of Starbucks were invisible to me. It felt like everyone was participating in a ritual that I was excluded from. I felt like an alien on the wrong planet.

Once I got up to the cashier to order my coffee, things got worse. The number of drink choices, all of them unfamiliar, was overwhelming. But that's beside the point. The worst part came when the team member asked me, "Do you want a Venti, a tall, or a grande?" What do any of those words mean in relation to coffee? How much is a tall? What is a Venti? How much coffee am I getting with a grande? Can I get a medium coffee?!

To this day, I hate Starbucks. It's a hellspot.

People with autism commonly have issues with sensory inputs. What's normal for the typical person might be too loud, too cold, too hot, too colorful, too stark, too itchy, too boomy, too whispery, or too soft. What's normal for a typical person might be hell for a person with autism.

Have you ever walked through a mall? That's hell to me.

Have you ever walked through a mall and an inconsiderate person sprays perfume in your face?

That's torturous hell for me.

Have you ever touched a sweater made of rabbit fur? That's cruel, and it's hell to me. Also, why would you turn a bunny rabbit into a sweater?

How do we, as middle-aged women with autism, deal with these modern hellspots?

My first choice is always to avoid these places and these things. There is no fighting how difficult it is for me. It can take me hours or days to recover from one of these experiences.

Over the years, especially with the Internet, I have developed several survival strategies. I will remind you, readers, that the first strategy for me is always to avoid these places in the first place.

When it comes to Starbucks, I prefer to make my coffee at home. If I must have coffee from Starbucks, I now make sure I order and pay for them online through my phone. That way all I must do is walk in briefly to pick up my coffee. I also make sure it's the same coffee shop each time. I don't like to experiment with new Starbucks.

I don't go shopping at the mall because that way lies madness. I prefer to do my shopping online. It is a privilege of living in this day and age and having access to disposable income. I really don't have another alternative. The mall sucks. Target sucks. Walmart is an M. Escher drawing come to life.

For many other circumstances and hellspots, I make sure I keep a few items on hand, just in case. I have noise canceling headphones in my purse all the time. I used to have very cheap earplugs that I carry with me everywhere I go. Nowadays, since I'm a mature professional career woman, I have a fancy new Air Pod Pro. With the fancy new Air Pod Pro, I can look like a thoughtless person listening to music, rather than an odd person with earplugs walking around in public.

Cove-19 is its own subject. One thing that came out of COVID-19 was the normalization of wearing masks. I always have one on hand. Besides giving me privacy, a.k.a., no one can see my face!!, a mask also blocks out a lot of smells. Best thing in the world! How did I ever get around without a mask before the pandemic?! I'm never going back! Have you been on an airplane prior to the pandemic? It was a hellspot! But now, with a mask, the smells are dulled! It's delightful!

Not every person with autism has sensory issues or sensitivity. If you do, there are many different strategies to help you cope with living in a neurotypical world that is full of hell spots for you. And if all else fails, do what I do, which is avoid at all costs.

6 HOW TO USE A MAP TO NAVIGATE TO YOUR LOCAL GROCERY STORE OR HOW TO USE ACCOMODATIONS TO MAKE YOUR LIFE EASIER

I have worked at the same school for five years now, and every morning when I get in my car, I turn on my navigation system and GPS my way to work. You would think, after five years, I would feel confident that I know how to get to work without using a GPS. Nevertheless, I don't feel confident. Every morning, I use GPS to drive the same route to work.

A couple of years ago, my husband had to undergo back surgery and could not drive. I drove him around for a couple of weeks. The first time I got behind the wheel of the car with him in the passenger seat was when I was taking him home from the hospital. The hospital was 3.2 miles away from our house, along the same big road that I drove to work every morning.

I got in the car, buckled up, turned to him and said, "How do we get home?"

He exclaimed, probably because he was still drugged, "We live three miles away! How do you not know how to get home from here?!"

My husband loves me and would normally never say anything like that. That's how I knew he was suffering. My loving husband knows that no matter where I am or where I'm going, I get lost.

There are some things I know a lot about and most everything else that I don't know anything about because I am not interested. We touched on this previously with the topic or special interest. It just so happens that navigation and directions are those things I'm not interested in, nor do I ever pay attention to. Rather than fighting my tendency to forget all directions and navigations, I make sure that I have a strategy to help me cope, meaning I always have access to GPS.

Remember back in the days of MapQuest?

Remember the days before with the Thomas Guide books? That was hell. I could not get anywhere without getting lost. There were numerous trips with me crying in the car on the side of the road because I got lost one more time. I hated driving for that reason. I hated traveling for that reason. If I could stay home all the time, I would. Now, with GPS, I feel more confident traveling in the neurotypical world.

This coping mechanism is called accommodation. The GPS, the Air Pod Pro, masks, and various other tools are all accommodations that help me make it through one more day on this alien planet.

No, I don't know if getting lost all the time is a characteristic of other middle-aged women with autism or if it's just me, but what I learned is that no matter what the issue is that I'm struggling with, some kind of accommodation can help me cope and perhaps, even thrive. What is your unique situation? What are some of your accommodations to help you survive on this weird, alien planet?

7 HOW TO HAVE FRIENDSHIPS AND ACQUAINTANCES AND REMEMBER THE NAMES OF THE MASSIVE SEA OF NAMELESS, FACELESS OTHER PEOPLE

In senior year in high school, Renata said "Best friends should dorm together. We should dorm together!"

That came as a complete surprise to me that I had a best friend. I still have a best friend. The same best friend. Mostly because she declared herself my best friend and I believed her. We shared a dorm room together in college and she became my lifeline and was really the person who taught me how to cope with living on an alien planet surrounded by alien people.

I used to be called cold and heartless. People either thought I did not like them or that I didn't care. It turned out that I cared very deeply but only about a few people. The people who thought I hated them? I did not have a relationship with them that I would consider significant or meaningful. This is a nice way of saying they didn't register in my awareness. I neither hated them nor liked them. I didn't know they were there.

Let's unravel some of this. People with autism have been accused repeatedly of not having emotions or sensitivity or empathy or sympathy. None of that is true to my knowledge. I have a tremendous amount of deep emotions. I love deeply. I hate deeply. I also don't care deeply. There's no part of my emotions that are mild or mellow. I feel the highs, I feel the lows, and where I don't feel much of anything, I absolutely feel not much of anything. In fact, it's hard for me to imagine other people just having mild feelings about anything. What does that mean to have mild feelings? You either are or you're not! How is a person supposed to be a little in love with someone? You either are or you're not.

People with autism have the full range of human emotions. We may have difficult processing, identifying, or talking about our emotions, but so do many neurotypical people. Think of "difficulty expressing emotions" as a star in the sky. Many constellations can have the same star as part of their patterns. It just so happens that many people with autism have that star in their constellation. That doesn't limit our ability to feel deeply about our family and friends or our desire for meaningful relationships.

Human beings are social animals with complex and interdependent social groups that help us survive and thrive. The smallest such social group is the family unit. In some cultures, that's a very small group consisting of parents and children, possibly even grandparents. In some cultures, the family group can be very extensive. Then, our social group expands beyond the immediate family to include friends, and then coworkers and acquaintances, perhaps a sports team or a religious group.

The idea of having a sports team or a religious group or any groups of the sort makes me want to lock my doors and windows and crawl under my blanket to hide from people.

My closest relationships are with a few people within my immediate family, including my husband, my sister, my cousin, and that's it. Those are my closest relationships. I have three close relationships. You read that right. I have three close relationships. Outside of that, I have relationships that are close, but not as close, with more members of my family, including other siblings, a few cousins, and Renata, my friend from high school. That's not very many. But it's more than I can manage on some days.

The next layer of my relationships are some people that I call "friends" but they're really on the same level as some of my coworkers that I enjoy working with. It's hard for me to differentiate my feelings between not-that-close friends or coworkers. Oftentimes, my coworkers are my not-that-close friends.

I treasure my very close relationships and I have very few of them.

It doesn't mean that I don't have emotions, sympathy, or empathy. It means that I feel deeply for a few people, and I don't spread my feelings to a large group of people. Spreading my feelings around too many people feels disingenuous and exhausting.

Most people are acquaintances to me. I even know some of their names. I don't know all their names. I remember some of their faces and, sometimes, I'm able to connect the faces with their names. I feel like that's not true of other people. I feel like other people would know who their acquaintances are. It took a while, but I'm OK with this. I no longer hold myself to the same expectations of having relationships like what's shown on TV.

How do I maintain relationships with my friends and family? Or at least the ones that I consider close relationships. When it comes to my Renata, I never call, I never text, but I also don't rely on her to maintain the relationship.

She often is the person who is actively maintaining our relationship. Whenever she is in town, she contacts me and makes me go out with her. That's usually once every two years since we live so far apart now. She calls me every few months and I always get a Christmas card.

Every other year, during my summer vacation, I make sure I do my "social rounds". I have family in Texas, my Renata in Minnesota, and my husband's family in Wisconsin. Every two years, I fly to Texas to see my Texas family members, then I fly to Minnesota and spend a few days with my best friend, then my husband meets me in Minnesota, and we drive together to Wisconsin to spend a few more days in Wisconsin with his family before flying home. That exhausts me, but then I don't have to think about talking to them or texting them or sending cards to them for another two years. That seems to work out well for all of us.

For my friends and family who are geographically near me, I rely on them to let me know when there's a social event that requires my presence. I really do try to attend as many of the family events as I possibly can, but nowadays, I have an uncountable number of nieces and nephews all under the age of 10 within a 40-minute drive. There are family events every other weekend. I can't do that. Just the thought of attending family events every two weekends exhausts me.

Instead, my family knows I try to see them every two months or so. My cousin Belle makes sure to let me know which events are the most important ones that I must attend. She periodically reminds me that Thanksgiving, though loud and smelly, is a family event that I must attend.

I am privileged to have close friends and family who know that I am a person with autism and that I struggle with certain things but that doesn't mean I don't love them or want to see them. I just want to see them for a limited amount of time occasionally.

To accommodate me, they communicate to me when it's important for me to show up. They also understand that I won't show up to most of the random events.

What can you do as a person with autism who wants to maintain close relationships with a few people around you? Communication is the key in this case. Let the people you want to maintain a close relationship with know exactly what you need from them and what you are capable of. Set boundaries, but don't forget that you can do some things to actively maintain your relationships.

8 HOW TO START A RELATIONSHIP WITH A SIGNIFICANT OTHER

Warning: *This chapter contains potentially disturbing content involving spousal abuse. Please take care of yourself. Feel free to skip this chapter.*

The second time I stood in front of the police officers with the back of my head slightly bleeding, my arms slightly bruised, I thought to myself, "I might not be alive for the third time."

The police officer looked at me and the look in his eyes said he already knew what my answer was going to be. He asked me, "Are you OK?"

I answered, "Yes, I am OK. My husband was just upset, but I am OK."

The look in his eyes said that he had seen this before many times, and he already knew that I was going to return to an abusive relationship from which I may not escape or survive.

I didn't want there to be a third time. I didn't want the police officer to look at me like that again.

That was the moment I finally recognized that I was in an abusive marriage.

People with disabilities have a much higher risk of being abused than people without disabilities. Regardless of gender, sexual orientation, or socioeconomic situation, people with disabilities have a much higher rate of being abused. I am a part of that statistics.

It took me a few more years to safely escape from that relationship. It took me months after my escape to finally begin divorce proceedings. The day my divorce finalized was the day I blocked my ex-husband's phone number and finally stopped receiving verbal abuse from him.

I want to pause here and say if you are in an abusive relationship or suspect you are, in the United States, we have the National Domestic Violence Hotline. The number is 1-800-799-7233 or

TTY 1-800-787-3224. You deserve to be safe. You deserve to be happy.

I got into this abusive relationship because I did not want to be rude. I did not want to be rude. And because I did not want to be rude, I ended up being verbally, physically, and financially abused. What a terrible trade off!

People with autism have difficulty interpreting, understanding, and navigating social relationships, norms, rituals, and conventions. In America, regardless of the ongoing fight against sexism, there are still sexist expectations of women to be amenable, nice, and polite to other people even when it makes them uncomfortable. Women with autism absolutely have a great deal of difficulty navigating relationship norms.

My first date with my ex went well. We had a good time. My second date with my ex went OK. I was only 22 at the time. I didn't have a great deal of expectations, I thought things were going well, and on the second date it likely was going well. On the third date, he got very drunk and as I was driving us home, he got very mad. While I was driving 65 miles an hour down the freeway, he opened the car door and threatened to kill himself because he was very mad that I wanted to go home instead of letting him continue drinking. I was shocked and I think I was shocked for the next few years. I didn't stop being shocked until I stood in front of that police officer for the second time.

What I could have done after dropping him off at his place was politely dump him. But I did not know how to do that without being rude. So, I did not. Instead, I continued dating him hoping it was a one-off. It was not. When he asked me to marry him, I was already in an abusive relationship, he had already moved in, and there was no way out at that point.

When my divorce finalized in my mid 30s, I was ecstatic and determined to enjoy every moment of my freedom. Happiness. I had forgotten what it felt like until then.

I became a superstar dater. In the early stages of dating apps, I could have as many dates as I wanted. Whenever I felt like having sushi for dinner, I would go on a date. My weekends were packed and many of my school nights were as well.

Remember, I was a fantastic flirter because I studied how to do it in college. I deployed all my flirtatious skills upon these poor unsuspecting men who were in their mid-30s and early 40s, well-established in their professional careers, with well-paying jobs, houses, and cars. I went on a spree of fantastic dates! I went to fancy restaurants! I drank expensive wine! I went on surprise weekend getaways to beach bungalows in Southern California! I got flown to the mountains of Montana for a weekend of hiking and nature. Whatever I wanted, I could have, in this new dating world.

What I did not want was another abusive relationship.

I made a list. It was an extensive list. It started with tall, handsome, intelligent, funny, well off, well spoken, well educated, family-centered, and mentally healthy, not an alcoholic, not abusive, not passive aggressive, and so on. Everything on that list was non-negotiable.

If I got so much as a hint that the person I was dating had self-esteem problems, I would politely decline the next date. If my date got pushy, I rudely declined the next date and blocked their phone number. If there was a hint of passive aggressiveness, I was gone. If there was a tiny whisper that family was not important to them, I was gone like a puff of smoke. Some of my dates lasted one date, some of my dates lasted two or three dates, only a rare few managed to last a few weeks.

I was quickly going through an extensive list of potential partners looking for someone who met my extremely high expectations. This was how I determined I was not going to be in an unhealthy relationship ever again. This was how I determined that I was going to find a healthy relationship for me. I set solid boundaries.

Six months after I started dating again, I saw this handsome man at a friend's gathering. Oh yes, I went to a few social gatherings. By that I meant, I went to two social gatherings. One of my coworkers was determined to help me find a partner. She dragged me to two house parties that her friends were hosting. At the second house party, a man walked by with broad, yummy shoulders and a slight swagger. I liked his broad shoulders. I watched him all night. I had to remind myself not to stare at him, but I didn't know what to do. I really liked his shoulders. It was getting towards the end of the evening and my friend and I were about to leave. I panicked.

I walked up to him, tapped him on his wide shoulders and asked, "Are you single?"

He paused and replied "Yes?"

I said "Here's my number. Call me."

Then, I walked away.

The next day, he called, and we started talking.

That was not my finest flirtation.

Six years later, we were married and living happily in suburban bliss.

It turned out he had also recently divorced from an abusive spouse. He was one of the lucky ones too. Coming out of our relationships, we both knew what we wanted, and what we didn't want. Our values and interests also matched up extremely well. Love came easily after that.

It wasn't long into our dating life that I told him that I'm a woman with autism who recently came out of a messy divorce. He understood. Over the years, he learned all sorts of different ways to make our lives happy. We communicated our different needs.

He worked to make space in our daily life so that I could be my authentic, autistic, and gifted self.

That meant texting with me for two months when the pandemic first began because I didn't feel like talking verbally. That meant shutting the doors and windows and handing me my Bose headphones when the neighbors started mowing their grass. That meant listening to me talk about all the different runs that I had to do to train for a marathon and never once acting like he wasn't interested. It also meant giving me weeks of notice when his parents came to visit. It also meant that I learned how to ride a bicycle for the first time in my life because it's something that he enjoyed. It meant taking trips to new places, even if I had to clutch his hands during take-offs and landings. It meant lots of adjustments in both of our lives.

Dating and relationships are complicated enough for the typical person. It becomes extremely difficult for women with autism and especially older women. I thought I might have some advice here, but I really don't because I barely survived one marriage. I may have lucked out with my second marriage.

I think it really helped that I knew exactly what I did want and exactly what I didn't want. It also helped that I was no longer afraid of saying no to what I do not want.

My last words on this matter, for anybody, whether you have an autistic diagnosis or not, don't prioritize politeness over your happiness. Don't be afraid to be rude.

9 CONCLUSION

The short e-book is already getting too long for me and yet there's a lot of topics I have not touched on. Stimming, repetitive motions that feel good to us. Preferences for strict routines. Eating. Ability to communicate verbally. Getting a job. Comorbidity with attention deficit, anxiety, or other conditions. Meltdowns or shutdowns. Raising children who may or may not have autism. The list goes on.

Research on autism has traditionally been focused on young male children. There's still a lot of research that needs to be done to fully understand people with autism. As of right now, older women with autism are least understood. I hope that this book contributes to our collective understanding of women with autism with the caveat that this e-book consists of a single person's experience.

Even though there are patterns of characteristics that make up the constellation of a person with autism, each individual person exhibits these characteristics in their own way. We know that the brains of people identified as autistic are different from the brains of people who are Neurotypical. We also know that people with autism have the full range of emotions and emotional needs that Neurotypical people do regardless of what characteristics they exhibit.

I wrote this book in the hopes that I can connect with other older women with autism. If you are an older person with autism you are welcome to connect with me and that in our shared experience we can support each other.

This is funny because as soon as I finish writing this book and publish it, I'm going to want to disappear. I never want to think about this book again or talk about this book again or allow my husband to read this book. Writing this e-book is cathartic for me, a part of my self-therapy to help me understand myself.

I'm one of the people who believe that autism is not a disease that needs to be cured. It's not an illness that we need to take a pill in order to alleviate the symptoms. I happen to believe that people with autism, people with ADHD, people with depression and anxieties, and all the people with different brains make up the full spectrum of humanity so that humanity is rich, diverse, inclusive, and beautiful. We are who we are and there's nothing wrong with us.

There is something wrong about us trying to fit into a world that is designed for Neurotypical brains and not for our brains. That's where conflicts can arise. That's why we have sensory overload and end up feeling drained, exhausted, or having a meltdown. I believe that if the world is designed to include the full spectrum of humanity, then we can all live comfortably and happily on this planet and perhaps it won't be so alien for some of us. Until that world arises, where all our needs are met whether we are at one end of the spectrum or the other end of the spectrum, it's up to us and our family and friends, sadly, that have to accommodate, fit and adjust into a world that is not designed for us.

ABOUT THE AUTHOR

Dr. Sefi Corner is a professional mask, a pseudonym for the author to protect her comfort level and her professional life. She is a middle-aged educator with 22 years of experience in public school as an elementary teacher and district-level professional development provider. This e-book is her first foray into non-fiction book publishing.

Contact the author at Sefi.Corner@gmail.com. Follow her on Twitter @DrSefiCorner